AMERICAN HOLIDAYS

★ ★

Thanksgiving Day

Barbara Balfour

Weigl Publishers Inc.

Published by Weigl Publishers Inc.
350 5th Avenue, Suite 3304, PMB 6G
New York, NY 10118-0069
Website: www.weigl.com

Library of Congress Cataloging-in-Publication Data

Balfour, Barbara.
  Thanksgiving day / Barbara Balfour.
      p. cm. -- (American holidays)
  Includes index.
  ISBN 1-59036-405-8 (hard cover : alk. paper) -- ISBN 1-59036-408-2 (soft cover : alk. paper)
  1. Thanksgiving Day--Juvenile literature. I. Title. II. American holidays (New York, N.Y.)
  GT4975.B35 2007
  394.2649--dc22

                          2005029036

Printed in the United States of America
1 2 3 4 5 6 7 8 9 0 10 09 08 07 06

Editor Heather C. Hudak
Design and Layout Terry Paulhus

Cover Thanksgiving Day began as a
harvest festival in autumn.

All of the Internet URLs given in the book were valid at the time of
publication. However, due to the dynamic nature of the Internet,
some addresses may have changed, or sites may have ceased
to exist since publication. While the author and publisher regret
any inconvenience this may cause readers, no responsibility for
any such changes can be accepted by either the author or
the publisher.

Every reasonable effort has been made to trace ownership and to
obtain permission to reprint copyright material. The publishers
would be pleased to have any errors or omissions brought to their
attention so that they may be corrected in subsequent printings.

Contents

Introduction

★ ★

Thanksgiving was first celebrated more than 370 years ago.

DID YOU KNOW?

Thanksgiving became an official national holiday in the United States in 1863.

Thanksgiving Day is a national holiday held on the fourth Thursday of November. It was first celebrated more than 370 years ago by the **pilgrims** and the **Wampanoag Indians**.

Americans celebrate Thanksgiving Day with family and friends. Many enjoy a large afternoon meal. The meal often includes corn, sweet potatoes, cranberries, and pumpkin pie. The main dish is often a big, stuffed turkey.

Thanksgiving is a day to give thanks for family, friends, shelter, food, and good health. It is also a day to remember what the pilgrims and Wampanoag Indians shared at their first Thanksgiving celebration.

4

Turkey has been part of Thanksgiving Day celebrations in the United States since the first Thanksgiving feast in 1621.

The Pilgrims Give Thanks

★ ★

The pilgrims celebrated their new land and freedom with a harvest festival.

DID YOU KNOW?

The pilgrim's first Thanksgiving meal included lobsters, eels, wild turkeys, geese, pumpkins, and grapes.

In 1620, a group of pilgrims sailed from Europe to the United States. They came on a ship called the *Mayflower*. The pilgrims settled in Plymouth, Massachusetts.

It was winter when the pilgrims first arrived. They had very little food to eat. Almost half of the pilgrims died.

Two Wampanoag Indians named Squanto and Samoset helped the pilgrims. They showed them how to farm their land and build homes.

By the next autumn, the pilgrims had food to eat and homes to live in. The pilgrims celebrated their new land and freedom with a harvest festival. They invited the Wampanoag Indians to eat with them. The celebration lasted for three days. This harvest festival is now called Thanksgiving.

Rejoice Together

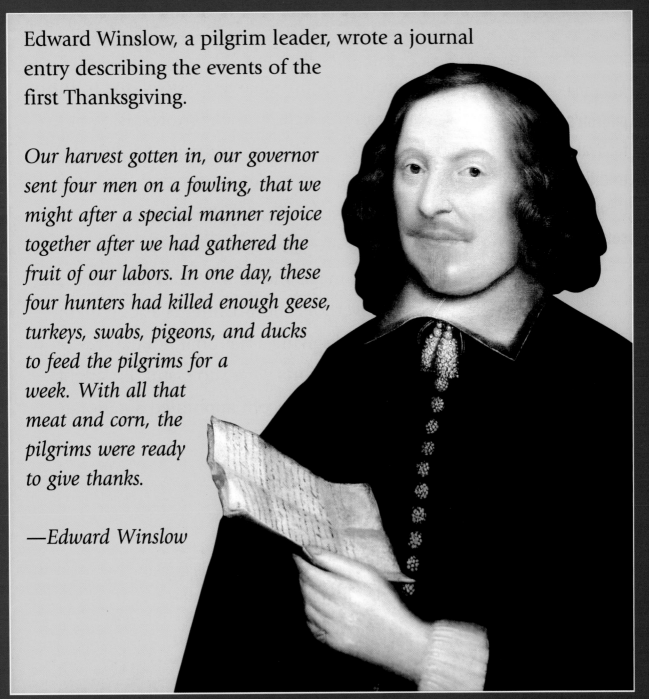

Edward Winslow, a pilgrim leader, wrote a journal entry describing the events of the first Thanksgiving.

Our harvest gotten in, our governor sent four men on a fowling, that we might after a special manner rejoice together after we had gathered the fruit of our labors. In one day, these four hunters had killed enough geese, turkeys, swabs, pigeons, and ducks to feed the pilgrims for a week. With all that meat and corn, the pilgrims were ready to give thanks.

—Edward Winslow

Edward Winslow wrote several books about the Plymouth colony and served three terms as governor.

Colonial Thanksgiving

★ ★

After the pilgrim's harvest festival, the tradition spread throughout the colonies.

After the pilgrim's harvest festival, the **tradition** spread throughout the **colonies**. Each of the colonies celebrated a day of thanks on different dates. October 1777 marked the first time all 13 colonies joined in a celebration together.

For 30 years, magazine editor Sarah Josepha Hale wrote to governors and **presidents** asking them to make Thanksgiving a national holiday. By 1863, Hale's efforts were successful. President Abraham Lincoln appointed a national day of thanksgiving.

★ ★ ★ ★ ★ ★ ★ ★ ★ ★

Sarah Josepha Hale helped make Thanksgiving Day a national holiday.

Original Thirteen Colonies of the United States

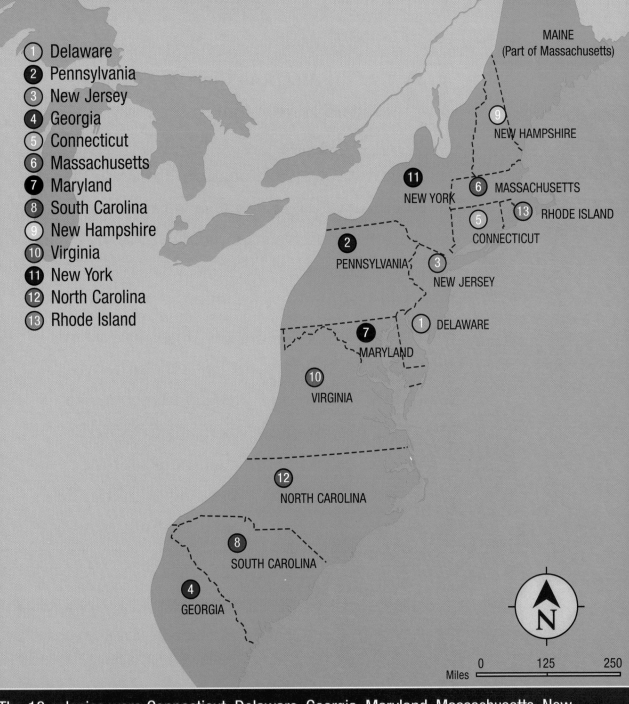

1. Delaware
2. Pennsylvania
3. New Jersey
4. Georgia
5. Connecticut
6. Massachusetts
7. Maryland
8. South Carolina
9. New Hampshire
10. Virginia
11. New York
12. North Carolina
13. Rhode Island

MAINE
(Part of Massachusetts)

9 NEW HAMPSHIRE

11 NEW YORK

6 MASSACHUSETTS

13 RHODE ISLAND

5 CONNECTICUT

2 PENNSYLVANIA

3 NEW JERSEY

1 DELAWARE

7 MARYLAND

10 VIRGINIA

12 NORTH CAROLINA

8 SOUTH CAROLINA

4 GEORGIA

N

0   125   250
Miles

The 13 colonies were Connecticut, Delaware, Georgia, Maryland, Massachusetts, New Hampshire, New Jersey, New York, North Carolina, Pennsylvania, Rhode Island, South Carolina, and Virginia.

Uniting a Nation

★ ★

President Abraham Lincoln called on Americans to express a day of thanks.

During the **American Civil War**, President Abraham Lincoln looked for a way to unite the nation. On October 3, 1863, he gave his Thanksgiving Day **proclamation**. President Lincoln called on Americans to unite "with one heart and one voice" to observe a special day of thanksgiving.

President Lincoln set aside the last Thursday of November for the holiday. He urged prayers in churches and in homes for "peace, harmony, tranquility, and union." President Lincoln also wanted Americans to express heartfelt thanks for the "blessing of fruitful fields and healthful skies."

★ ★ ★ ★ ★ ★ ★ ★ ★ ★
By the middle of the nineteenth century, 29 states celebrated an annual Thanksgiving Day meal.

After President Abraham Lincoln's proclamation, Thanksgiving became an annual national holiday.

Creating the Holiday

★ ★

More than 250,000 people watched Macy's first Thanksgiving parade.

George Washington was the first president to set aside November 26 for a day of giving thanks. It was not until 1941 that **Congress** created a law making Thanksgiving Day a national holiday on the fourth Thursday of November.

Macy's Department Store in New York City held its first Thanksgiving parade in 1924. The store's employees marched on 34th Street with floats, live bands, and animals. More than 250,000 people watched the parade. It was such a huge success that Macy's made it a yearly event.

★ ★ ★ ★ ★ ★ ★ ★ ★
George Washington's Thanksgiving Day proclamation called for a day to honor the creation of the United States government, as well as to give thanks and praise.

Macy's Thanksgiving Day Parade includes popular cartoon balloons, such as Underdog, Bullwinkle, Superman, Snoopy, and Garfield.

Celebrating Today

Thanksgiving is a day of feasting with family and friends.

American families celebrate Thanksgiving Day with yearly traditions. The most common tradition is the gathering of family and friends. They share a large afternoon meal together. Other traditions on this holiday vary from family to family.

Some families watch parades in their towns and cities. Other people watch the annual Thanksgiving Championship. This is a major football game between the two best college teams in the country.

Some families celebrate the holiday by going to church. Before eating their big meal, they say a special prayer to give thanks for their blessings.

DID YOU KNOW?

Thanksgiving in the United States is a four-day holiday. Americans are given Thursday and Friday off from work and school to celebrate the occasion.

At Plimoth Plantation in Massachusetts, actors and actresses dress in traditional pilgrim clothing and perform activities to show what life was like in the 1600s.

On Thanksgiving Day, some people give back to the community by preparing and serving meals.

Americans Celebrate

Americans celebrate Thanksgiving with a four-day holiday. Thanksgiving Day traditions include a large meal, parades, festivals, and college or professional football games.

For some people in San Francisco, California, turkey is not the main dish on Thanksgiving Day. There are people who enjoy Dungeness crab as the main dish. The crab season begins in November.

San Francisco, California

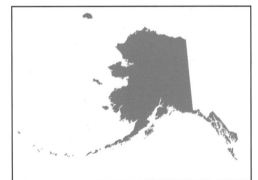

0 100 200 300 miles

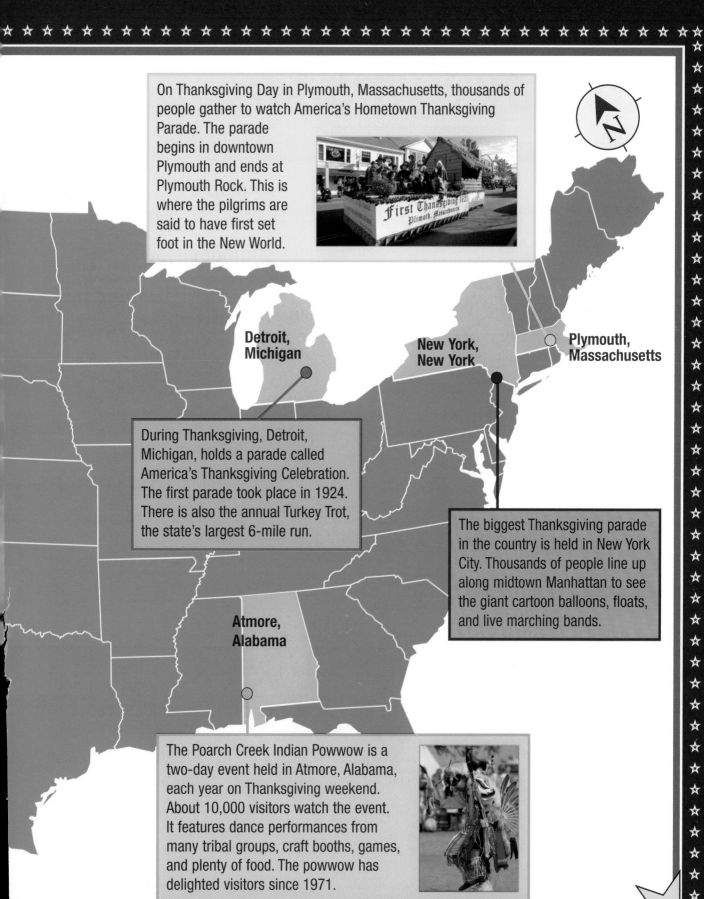

On Thanksgiving Day in Plymouth, Massachusetts, thousands of people gather to watch America's Hometown Thanksgiving Parade. The parade begins in downtown Plymouth and ends at Plymouth Rock. This is where the pilgrims are said to have first set foot in the New World.

First Thanksgiving 1621
Plimoth, Massachusetts

Detroit, Michigan

New York, New York

Plymouth, Massachusetts

During Thanksgiving, Detroit, Michigan, holds a parade called America's Thanksgiving Celebration. The first parade took place in 1924. There is also the annual Turkey Trot, the state's largest 6-mile run.

The biggest Thanksgiving parade in the country is held in New York City. Thousands of people line up along midtown Manhattan to see the giant cartoon balloons, floats, and live marching bands.

Atmore, Alabama

The Poarch Creek Indian Powwow is a two-day event held in Atmore, Alabama, each year on Thanksgiving weekend. About 10,000 visitors watch the event. It features dance performances from many tribal groups, craft booths, games, and plenty of food. The powwow has delighted visitors since 1971.

Holiday Symbols

When people think of Thanksgiving, many think of food. While food is an important part of the holiday, there are many other symbols that make the holiday a special occasion. Here are some of the key symbols of Thanksgiving.

Cornucopia

The cornucopia is also known as the Horn of Plenty. It symbolizes wealth and good fortune. In ancient times, the cornucopia was a goat's horn filled with fruits and flowers. Today, it is used as a Thanksgiving symbol. The cornucopia is displayed as a horn-shaped wicker basket filled with fruits and vegetables.

In Ancient Greece, many people believed the cornucopia was a special horn that could be filled with anything the owner wished.

Turkey

Turkeys are only found in North America. They were among the first foods the pilgrims ate when they came to the United States. Wild turkeys were more common then. **Benjamin Franklin** wanted the wild turkey to be the national bird of the United States. The national bird became the bald eagle.

Cranberries

Cranberries were part of the first Thanksgiving celebration. The Wampanoag Indians called the fruit *ibimi,* meaning "bitter berry." The Wampanoag Indians taught the pilgrims to cook the berries with a sweetener to make a sauce. The pilgrims renamed the fruit "crane-berry" because its flowers looked like a bird called a crane. Today, cranberries are grown all over New England on the northeastern coast.

Further Research

You can find more information about Thanksgiving Day by reading the following books and visiting the following websites.

Websites

To find out more about Thanksgiving Day traditions, visit:
www.thanksgiving-traditions.com

To learn more about the history of Thanksgiving Day, visit:
www.historychannel.com/ thanksgiving

Books

Ballam, Anthea. *Mayflower: The Voyage that Changed the World.* Oakland, CA: O Books, 2003.

Grippo, Robert M. and Christopher Hoskins. *Macy's Thanksgiving Day Parade.* Mount Pleasant, SC: Arcadia Publishing, 2004.

Crafts and Recipes

Turkey Treats

You will need:
an oval cracker
canned frosting
a chocolate kiss
candy corn
a caramel

1. Spread frosting on a cracker.
2. Peel the paper off the chocolate kiss, and place the kiss near the bottom of the cracker.
3. Add candy corn above the kiss to make feathers.
4. Place one corn on the kiss for the head.
5. Let the frosting dry.
6. Attach a caramel to the back of the cracker with more frosting to make it stand up.

Thanksgiving Day Craft

Pilgrim Puppets

Materials:

2 toilet paper rolls	felt	pen or pencil
construction paper	glue	scissors
craft sticks	moving eyes	yarn

1. Cover the toilet tissue roll with black paper.
2. Cut a 2-inch circle out of white construction paper. Draw a face on it. Then, glue it onto the top side of the toilet tissue roll.
3. To make a pilgrim boy, add a black hat with a white band and a buckle using construction paper or felt. Make a bow tie with yarn.
4. To make a pilgrim girl, add a white apron and hat using construction paper and felt. Make a bow on her hat with yarn.
5. Using scrap paper or felt, make hair, arms, and legs. Add the moving eyes.
6. Glue a craft stick inside the bottom edge of the cardboard roll for the puppet handle.
7. You can also make turkeys this way. Be creative and have fun!

Holiday Quiz

What have you learned about Thanksgiving Day? See if you can answer the following questions. Check your answers on the next page.

1 What year was the first Thanksgiving harvest festival?

2 When is Thanksgiving held in the United States?

3 What are three key symbols of Thanksgiving?

4 Who helped make Thanksgiving Day a national holiday?

5 Who were the two Wampanoag Indians who helped the pilgrims?

On Thanksgiving Day in Plymouth, Massachusetts, groups of people march down Court Street dressed as pilgrims, patriots, and pioneers.

Fascinating Facts

★ The pilgrims ate their biggest meal at noon. It was called noonmeat or dinner. The women spent part of their morning cooking that meal. They had a smaller meal at the end of the day. The pilgrims ate leftovers for breakfast.

★ More than 1 million people from all over the world visit Plymouth, Massachusetts, and Plymouth Rock each year.

★ More than 45 million turkeys are eaten each Thanksgiving Day in the United States.

★ There are three cities in the United States named after the turkey. Cities named Turkey are found in Texas and North Carolina. The town of Turkey Creek is found in Louisiana.

Quiz Answers:
1. The first Thanksgiving harvest festival was in 1621.
2. Thanksgiving Day is held on the fourth Thursday in November.
3. The three key symbols of Thanksgiving are the turkey, the cornucopia, and cranberries.
4. Sarah Josepha Hale helped make Thanksgiving Day a national holiday.
5. The two Wampanoag Indians were Squanto and Samoset.

Glossary

★ ★ ★ ★ ★ ★ ★ ★ ★ ★ ★ ★ ★ ★ ★

American Civil War: military conflict between the northern and southern states from 1861 to 1865

Benjamin Franklin: a well-known American inventor and scientist

colonies: territories

Congress: the national government of the United States

pilgrims: British travelers who journeyed to the United States in 1620

presidents: leaders of the United States government

proclamation: formal statement

tradition: a custom or way of doing something every year

Wampanoag Indians: American Indians who lived in Massachusetts long before the pilgrims arrived

Index

★ ★ ★ ★ ★ ★ ★ ★ ★ ★ ★ ★ ★ ★ ★ ★